BUNKER HILL
IN THE
REARVIEW MIRROR

The Rise, Fall,
and Rise Again of
an Urban Neighborhood

photo
friends

Los Angeles Public Library

Contents

Opposite: Built in 1887, the St. Angelo Hotel (Curlett, Eisen & Cuthbertson) dominated the corner of Temple and Grand for over seventy years. Once the destination of high society visitors to the city, the hotel eventually operated as a boarding house, gradually falling into disrepair. The building was vacated in 1956 under an order from the board of health and was ultimately demolished to make way for the Music Center. 1939. (Security Pacific National Bank Collection)

Introduction

by CHRISTINA RICE and EMMA ROBERTS

During its history, the area of Downtown Los Angeles known as Bunker Hill has been viewed in many different ways; inaccessible, upscale, run-down, blighted, erased, renewed. These perceptions over the decades have always been open to interpretation and either agreed with or challenged. An area that has been subject to more change than any other place in the city, it has arguably invoked more passion and reverence than any other Los Angeles neighborhood, while inspiring equal amounts of disdain.

The name Bunker Hill may have been bestowed in honor of the 100th anniversary of the Revolutionary War battle fought in Boston, or possibly because soldiers of the California Bear Flag Republic dug a series of bunkers into the crest of the hill during the Mexican War. As Los Angeles grew beyond the original Pueblo, Bunker Hill was seen as a risky development prospect because its elevation made the delivery of building materials and water

Opposite: Opened in 1904, the Touraine Apartments (A.L. Haley) brought elegant, yet compact living to a neighborhood noted for its Victorian mansions. The cleverly designed and patented floor plan squeezed the amenities of multiple rooms into only two, with features like Murphy Beds, bookcases built into closet doors, and a dining room table that could be folded and hung up. Standing four stories at the entrance, the Touraine dipped down an additional four floors towards the rear with the natural slope of the Hill. 1951. (Leonard Nadel/Housing Authority Collection)

Pages 4-5: In this long view of Bunker Hill, about 1890, the Crocker mansion's verandas are visible in the upper right. The home of L. J. Rose, a pioneer agricultural promoter and racehorse investor, is in the middle distance. But the photograph also finds many small cottages and modest homes as well as the mansions. The First Congregational Church is in the lower right corner, at Third and Hill. Ca 1890. (Security Pacific National Bank Collection)

The Bonaventure Hotel (1976) sharing space with The Engstrum Apartment Hotel (1914). Located at 623 W. 5th Street, the Engstrum survived the waves of redevelopment and seemed poised for longevity when a major renovation was announced in 1978. However, the building, which reportedly housed Charlie Chaplin and Rudolph Valentino during its long history, eventually made way for the 73-story Library Tower (1989, now known as the U.S. Bank Tower). 1980. (William Reagh Collection)

seemingly impossible. None of this discouraged developer Prudent Beaudry, who in 1867 saw nothing but potential and eventually brought roads and water to the Hill.

By the 1880s, Bunker Hill was decorated with Queen Anne and East-lake style residences where Downtown's doctors, lawyers, and merchants resided among others. It was a picturesque and comfortable neighborhood that became considerably more accessible with the opening of the Angels Flight incline railway in 1901. As the city continued its expansion, grand homes sprang up elsewhere, while Bunker Hill's mansions and hotels were converted into boarding houses, providing the working class, along with pensioners and artists, with long-term housing. Throughout the first half of the twentieth century, Bunker Hill may no longer have been upscale, but it was still a living and breathing neighborhood.

As the high-maintenance Victorian structures decayed, Bunker Hill gradually assumed a weather-worn appearance and later experienced an increase in crime, causing it to be labeled a slum in some circles. However, it also remained a vibrant neighborhood, inspiring novelists and filmmakers, many of whom used the neighborhood as a backdrop in their storytelling. A 1945 state redevelopment act paved the way for tax money to be used for the over-hauling of run-down urban areas, and despite the strong community that still existed, "blighted" came to be the term most associated with Bunker Hill by city officials.

With the formation of the Community Redevelopment Agency (CRA) in 1949, Bunker Hill became the first target for mass redevelopment. As feasibility reports were compiled and master plans drawn, landowners and residents of the neighborhood scaled their own Battle of Bunker Hill in order to stop the evictions and demolitions. In the end, redevelopment won. In an unprecedented move, most of the buildings on the Hill were razed, starting in the early 1960s. The natural landscape was also altered as man-made mechanics moved the earth and lowered the elevation, taking with it layers of local history. However, despite master plans and good intentions, much of the area

remained undeveloped in subsequent decades, with much of the leveled and vacant acreage serving as parking lots.

Gradually, Bunker Hill did rise again, at least literally, with the construction of numerous high rise office buildings, though it has arguably fallen short of the original vision of a vibrant live/work neighborhood. With vacant lots finally being developed and the gradual emergence of cultural institutions like the Museum of Contemporary of Art (MOCA), Disney Hall and the Broad Museum joining the Music Center, the promise of Bunker Hill laid out over half a century ago creeps closer.

When the old Bunker Hill neighborhood became endangered, photographers, artists, and reporters flocked to the area to capture its details and spirit before it vanished. Many of these photographs, paintings, news articles, recollections, and the printed reports from those responsible for its redevelopment have fortunately found their way to institutions like the Los Angeles Public Library. While they may not be able to tell the whole complex story of Bunker Hill, these artifacts at least give us a view of this part of the city in the rear view mirror. ⅋

Bunker Hill residences known as the "Salt Box" and "The Castle" are dwarfed by the recently constructed Union Bank Building. 1968. (William Reagh Collection)

THE CASTLE TIME LAPSE. Possibly the most photographed of the great Bunker Hill mansions, the structure located at 325 S. Bunker Hill and known as "The Castle" has come to visually exemplify the lost neighborhood of a bygone era. Built circa 1888, most likely by capitalist Reuben M. Baker, the Queen Anne style residence boasted 20 rooms, both a marble and a tile fireplace, and a three story staircase winding up the center of the house. Two of the mansion's most recognizable features were the stained-glass front door and an overhang on the north side for carriages to pass through to the rear of the property. In 1894, grading contractor Daniel F. Donegan purchased the property for $10,500 and moved in with his wife Helen and four children. Though the family lived there for less than ten years, the name Donegan became the one most associated with the house and it has long been believed that the clan were the ones who nicknamed the mansion "The Castle."

From left: "The Castle" in all its Victorian glory around the turn of the 20th century. The carriage sitting in front is decorated for the La Fiesta de las Flores parade. The next view shows the mansion, circa 1924 when it was run as a boarding house by Charles and Bertha Merrifeld. By 1965 when the third view was taken, the structure was missing the curved Mansard roof on the tower and the triangular crown of a front balcony, both casualties of the 1933 Long Beach earthquake. At the time, it was still being operated as a boarding house by the family of Gordon Pattison, who had owned it since the 1930s, although "The Castle's" days were numbered, as indicated by the artists on the front lawn, capturing the building on canvas while it was still standing. Finally, "the Castle" is shown elevated and in two pieces, awaiting its relocation to Heritage Square in the Montecito Heights neighborhood along with the neighboring "Salt Box." After surviving redevelopment and relocation, "The Castle" was lost in an arson fire in October 1969.

ANGELS FLIGHT TIME LAPSE. Four views near 3rd and Hill Streets present four completely different landscapes over the course of a century.

From left: From left: Looking west on 3rd towards Hill Street, circa 1886 shows a tranquil, tree-filled neighborhood. Visible in the distance is the Crocker Mansion which dominated the corner of 3rd and Olive Streets from 1886-1908, as well as the First Congregational Church in the right foreground. The introduction of the Angels Flight funicular and the 3rd Street Tunnel, both in 1901, provided ways to easily traverse Bunker Hill and the area started to take on a more concrete feel. The second view, circa 1935, shows the hustle and bustle on the sidewalks and streets, along with businesses and the myriad of rooming houses creeping up the Hill. By 1965, redevelopment was well under way. This is apparent in the third view which shows the two cars of Angels Flight, named *Sinai* and *Olivet*, making their short journeys through a barren landscape. Finally, this 1986 image shows an unrecognizable intersection. The Third Street Tunnel still exists, but is practically camouflaged by the Angelus Plaza (1980), an affordable housing community for seniors. Missing is Angels Flight, the funicular railway that had been financed by Colonel J.W. Eddy and ran continuously from 1901 until it was dismantled in 1969. Angels Flight was ultimately rebuilt a half a block north of its original location in 1996, though accidents in 2001 and 2013 have marred the return of this beloved Bunker Hill landmark.

PART I
Early Suburb

by MERRY OVNICK

The Pueblo of Los Angeles, founded in 1781 as a remote colonial outpost of New Spain, was originally located near the river. After a flood in 1815, the plaza was relocated to its present site[1] and Angelenos built their homes and businesses in the flatlands between the Los Angeles River and the lee of a hill that later came to be called Bunker Hill. The hill itself was slow to be settled.

In the era of horse-drawn transportation the hills on the western edge of town discouraged development. An 1849 survey made after the American acquisition of California shows Hill Street going no farther north than a point between Second and Third streets, and this was still the case in an 1875 map of the city.[2] An 1877 birds-eye view shows the steep ravines that made it even less attractive for settlement. Only a handful of houses could be found on the town side of the hill; an occasional farmhouse and orchard on the far side.[3] But in 1886-1887, a massive boom exploded the town of 11,000 into a city of 50,000[4] and real estate developers laid out a grid of streets and promoted property on the hill – so close to business, if inconveniently above it. Wealthy homeowners could commute by carriage; less wealthy climbed.

The 1888 Sanborn Fire Insurance Maps show the new homes cropping up on the eastern side of the hill, facing downtown. Some were, indeed, mansions, most colorfully that of Comstock Lode investor Lewis Bradbury, soon followed by other elaborate piles for Leonard J. Rose, Mrs. Edwin Bryant Crocker, and those of new wealth made in the Los Angeles boom. The popular notion of Bunker Hill as a redoubt of the wealthy is, however, not completely

Opposite: Architect John Hall constructed a huge home for Mrs. Edwin Bryant Crocker, widow of State Supreme Court Justice E. B. Crocker (simultaneously the counsel of the Central Pacific Railroad), at Olive and Third Streets in 1886. The steep bluff behind the house was luxuriously landscaped. In later years the house became a boarding house, then was replaced by an Elks lodge. (Security Pacific National Bank Collection)

Pages 16-17: In this 1891 view of the Hill, we can see the retaining walls and erosion that reflected the challenges to construction. The nearly-completed Bradbury mansion is in the upper right. 1891. (Security Pacific National Bank Collection)

An 1877 birds-eye panorama of Los Angeles, with Bunker Hill in the center foreground. The small town of Los Angeles celebrated its 1876 rail connection to San Francisco (see train on left). The town had grown southward from its old Spanish-era plaza (circle, left of center). But Bunker Hill (center foreground), cut by ravines and inconveniently steep for building, remained the site of scattered farms and an orchard. 1877. (E. L. Glover. Lithograph, A. L. Bancroft, Publisher)

accurate. Mansions make it into the photographic record; cottages rarely do. So it overturns our suppositions to see on the 1888 Sanborn map that duplexes, small single-story cottages, hotels, and boarding houses occupy lots on the same blocks as the 2½-story grand mansions with their gazebos and carriage barns. This map also indicates twenty- and thirty-foot banks, a deep valley between Olive and Grand, and a steep ravine between Second and Third. Portions of First Street and Hope Street are marked "Not graded, Impassable for vehicles." All the houses except one tiny duplex were wooden and there was one fire bell next to the single "electric light mast" on First Street between Olive and Hill Streets. At Courthouse (later, Court) Street, a long flight of stairs descended from Bunker Hill to the flatlands of downtown Los Angeles, passing in front of the Crocker mansion and a "furnished rooms" neighbor on Third Street between Olive and Clay.[5]

During the 1880s boom, some 200,000 visitors registered with the post office for window mail delivery.[6] They had to lodge somewhere, so boarding houses, furnished rooms, and hotels were good investments. After the boom, in the 1890s and into the early 1900s, they revived and multiplied as businesses drew clerks, stenographers, and typists—and did not pay them well enough to become home-owners.[7] The Melrose, built on Grand Avenue at Second as a private home in 1889, became an upscale boarding house, later connected to The Richelieu Hotel next door as an annex. Their well-dressed residents gathered for a group photograph in 1894.

The 1894 Sanborn maps find fewer empty lots on the hill. Some houses have been built on the rims of the steep valleys, supported "on posts 12′ high, open under"; some blocks are terraced; and retaining walls have proliferated. Almost all of the structures were wooden, but fire alarms appear at several intersections. "Lawn tennis courts" occupy a lot high above Hill Street.[8] In 1901 the long staircase down the hill at Third Street was supplemented by Angels Flight, an incline railway 315-feet long that took passengers up the hill from the flats for 1¢. In 1905 a rival Court Flight opened a couple of blocks north, connecting Court Street above to Broadway below. The Third Street Tunnel opened in 1901, enabling horse-drawn and the growing number of

This view, taken from the observation deck at the top of Angel's Flight in 1906 shows downtown Los Angeles, a bustling city of over 102,000 by 1900, growing to 319,000 by 1910. The left-hand scene is dominated by the county courthouse, completed in 1905. The dark structure with the tower to the left in the center image was the 1880s city hall, on

Broadway between Second and Third. The large building on the right, with the tent-like glass roof, is the Bradbury Building, completed in 1893 and still in use. A smokestack in the manufacturing area near the Los Angeles River belches smoke, then the proud sign of modern industry. 1906. (Security Pacific National Bank Collection)

At the southern foot of Bunker Hill, stood Central Park (now Pershing Square), across Olive Street from St. Paul's Episcopal Church. The Biltmore Hotel would be constructed to the right of the church in 1922. In the foreground, Sixth Street is to the left, intersected by Hill Street on the right. In the distance to the left is the State Normal School, a teacher-training institution that opened in 1882 and later became the Southern Branch of the University of California, the parent of UCLA. Ca 1886. (Security Pacific National Bank Collection)

horseless carriages to avoid climbing the hill altogether. Court Flight burned in 1943; Angels Flight closed in 1969 and was later relocated a few hundred feet south.[9] And all the houses on Bunker Hill are no more. ❧

After the 1886-87 real-estate boom, Bunker Hill bristled with elaborate Victorian mansions. One of the grandest was that of Lewis Bradbury, who had made his money in the Comstock Load. It was designed by Joseph Cather Newsom and located above Hill Street at Court (then Court House) Street. Bradbury also built an office building at Third and Broadway, the Bradbury Building (1893), still a breathtaking monument, with its glass roof and wrought iron décor. Next to Bradbury's house was one of the few electric light mast on the hill. This 1890s photo includes what looks like a telephone pole. Ca 1890s (Security Pacific National Bank Collection)

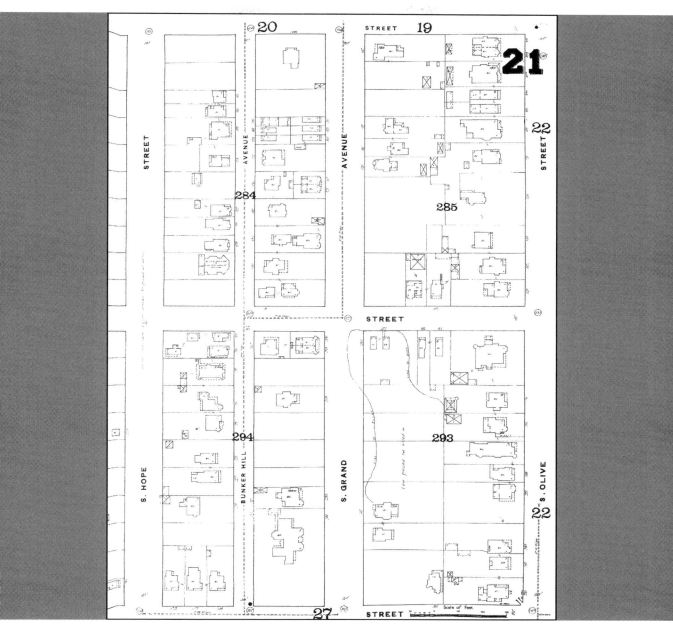

1888 Sanborn Map. This portion of the 1888 Sanborn Fire Insurance Map records the structures on Bunker Hill at that time. Almost all were wooden, yet there was only one fire bell at Court and Hill. It is clear from the map that this was not merely a retreat for the wealthy. Small cottages, duplexes, hotels and boarding houses sit side-by-side with the turreted mansions. The map also reveals the twenty- and thirty-foot banks and deep valleys that made some properties unbuildable. Yet planners of the time had platted streets on a grid.

A row of modest homes on Hill Street near Third, at the base of Bunker Hill. The Crocker mansion is at top center. 1886. (Security Pacific National Bank Collection)

A growing number of hotels and boarding houses were also to be found on Bunker Hill. In the 1880s Boom, trainloads of tourists and potential real-estate customers poured into town and investors found it profitable to establish hotels. The Melrose (left), by architect Joseph Cather Newsom at 138 S. Grand, was built as a private residence around 1889, but was later converted to serve as an annex of the Richelieu Hotel (right). Ca 1889. (Security Pacific National Bank Collection)

By the 1880s, a few wealthy Angelenos were constructing their mansions on the Hill.
Judge Anson Brunson, formerly counsel for the Atchison, Topeka and Santa Fe Railroad,
moved into his home at 347 S. Grand Avenue, and designed by Abram Edelman, in 1888.
(Security Pacific National Bank Collection)

The residents of the Melrose about 1894. By this time it was a respectable boarding house for young white-collar workers, some single, some with spouses and children. Ca 1894. (Security Pacific National Bank Collection)

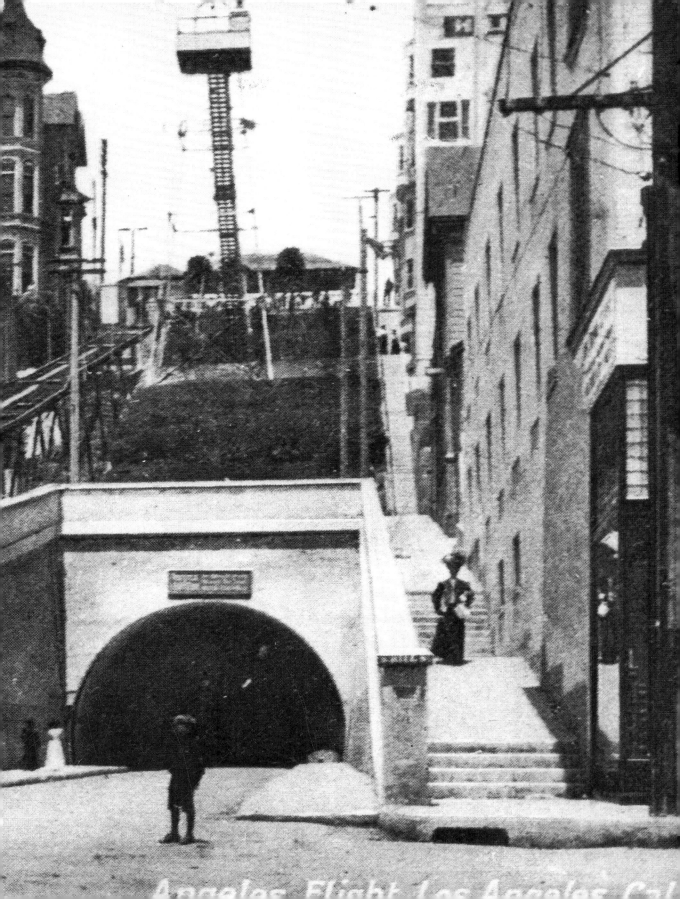

Angels Flight Los Angeles, Cal.

Overleaf: Those residents of Bunker Hill who owned a carriage might take a circuitous route down to their businesses or shopping in the flatland of downtown Los Angeles. The others trudged long staircases. In 1901 entrepreneur Col. J. W. Eddy opened Angel's Flight, a funicular railway that took passengers up or down the Hill at Third Street for only 1¢. The former Crocker mansion, by this time a boarding house, is at top center, an observation platform to its right. Angel's Flight was disassembled in 1969; reconstructed half a block away in 1995. It is currently closed. Ca 1903. (Security Pacific National Bank Collection)

A second short rail line was extended from Bunker Hill to the flatlands in 1905. Court Flight ran from Court Street on the Hill, down to Broadway, between Temple and First. A fire in 1943 ended its long run. In this 1918 photograph, we can see the stairs to the left of the tracks, for those unwilling to pay to ride. 1918. (Security Pacific National Bank Collection)

Opposite: Another view of Court Flight captured by Ansel Adams while on an assignment for *Fortune* magazine in 1940. The city had changed dramatically by that time; the older houses on the Hill had merely grown older. 1940. (Ansel Adams Collection)

CALIFORNIA STATE NORMAL SCHOOL   Los Angeles

A 1904 panorama of the students and faculty of the State Normal School at Fifth and Grand, now the location of the Los Angeles Central Library. Los Angeles promoters and residents in general embraced palm trees and other exotic tropical landscaping as they gloried in the Southern California climate. 1904. (C.C. Pierce & Co./Security Pacific National Bank Collection)

PART II

Flourishing
Neighborhood

by Nathan Marsak

The common conception about life on Bunker Hill involves grifters and b-girls, hopheads and ne'er-do-wells of every stripe, amid dank alleyways and gingerbread mansions casting deep shadows.

Bunker Hill exists as such in the popular imagination largely due to depictions in the romantic fiction of Fante, or the hardboiled prose of Chandler, whose bleak portrayal of its surroundings and denizens (women with "faces like stale beer" and men "with pulled-down hats and quick eyes") has become so ubiquitous as to define it. These, and the canon of *films noir* have led many to believe that Bunker Hill was ground zero for violence, despair, and a dark blur between good and evil.

Relatedly, predemolition Bunker Hill had its detractors—the Los Angeles *Times*, the CRA, and images by Leonard Nadel, photographer for the Los Angeles Housing Authority from 1949–1952, who portrayed it disparagingly. Statistics "proving" the Hill to be a reprobate area were touted repeatedly.

Bunker Hill residents countered with a quite different portrait: they asserted that their buildings were safe for occupancy, not conducive to ill health, disease, juvenile delinquency, infant mortality or crime. The Bunker Hill Property Owners Association passed a resolution against the taking of their property at condemnation prices, which would "entail a tremendous amount of loss, grief and trouble…the only crime of which our people can be safely charged, is hanging clothes to dry in a back yard."[1]

Opposite: Three elderly gentlemen socialize on a bench on top of the Hill Street Tunnel, looking south. The intersection seen below at street level is where 1st Street (only partially visible) meets Hill Street. 1940. (Ansel Adams Collection)

Pages 40-41: Running from 4th to 2nd Streets, in between Olive and Hill, Clay Street was more like an alley. Its run-down charm, lack of traffic, and occasional view of Angels Flight passing through made Clay Street a popular location with filmmakers who featured it in film such as *Act of Violence* (1949), *Once a Thief* (1950), *The Glenn Miller Story* (1953), *Kiss Me Deadly* (1955), and *The Exiles* (1961). When the area was redeveloped, Clay Street was completely erased from the landscape. 1960. (William Reagh Collection)

Certainly, Bunker Hill harbored the marginalized element—immigrants, homosexuals, Hispanics, the odd narcotics user, and a great many pensioners, whom we today might term the elderly poor. Among the populace lived some of LA's most unorthodox folk: noted esoteric mystics Max Heindel & Augusta Foss, founders of the Rosicrucian Fellowship, lived and worked at 315 S. Bunker Hill; the notorious Blackburn Cult began in 1922 at 355 S. Grand; important Modernist photographer and totemic bohemian Margrethe Mather kept her studio at 715 W 4th; and 221 S. Bunker Hill was a touchstone of early gay rights advocacy, where the articles of incorporation for One, Inc. were drafted.

Painters famously documented the Hill and her homes during its final days. Benjamin Abril became well-known for capturing Bunker Hill in his trademark luminous style. Leo Politi produced an entire book of watercolors dedicated to the Hill and her residents. Catherine "Kay" Martin was known as "The Vagabond of Bunker Hill," as she used her white station wagon as a portable painting studio. Marcel Cavalla, who had been a resident of the Brousseau Mansion at 238 S. Bunker Hill for twenty-three years, and had depicted the neighborhood on canvas for as long, was discovered by Politi.

Recently discovered amateur photographs, many in color, challenge the conventional understanding of the Hill as promulgated by the Housing Authority's Nadel, who made a point of shooting the ramshackle backyards, the shoeless children, the hanging laundry. Rather, many structures appear well-tended, and surrounded by flowers. A particular image of an elderly woman named Rose, of 246 S. Bunker Hill Avenue, tending to a neighborhood cat, mirrors a watercolor by Leo Politi as featured in his 1964 *Bunker Hill, Los Angeles: Reminiscences of Bygone Days.*

Nevertheless, there was a timeworn element to the neighborhood, owing only in part to the fashionable folk having once made their inexorable march to the sea. Largely, it was because talk of razing Bunker Hill dated back to the 'teens, and was set into motion after the passage of the 1945 Community Redevelopment Act. Properties went into decline as owners deferred maintenance. With the threat of condemnation and razing hanging over, why bother with upkeep?

The Hill had also become topographically isolated over the years, as tunnels burrowed through her. Auto ownership on the Hill was slight. Gordon Pattison, whose family owned several structures on the Hill, including the legendary Castle, and the Salt Box, provides a first-hand account of Hill life in the 1950s. He describes it as a haven of quietude, where the cooing of pigeons was more audible than the rush of the city below.

Ironically, life on Bunker Hill embodied much currently vaunted by planners: in reusing buildings instead of building new, the Hill was "green"; its mix of residential and commercial, along with its inherent "walkability," tags it as New Urbanist; and while once City fathers condemned Bunker Hill for being "too dense," today's City strategists engineer ways to increase density. Life on Bunker Hill should be mourned not only as a relic of the past, but because it was so ahead of its time. ❧

Laundry belonging to
residents of Bunker Hill
dries in the sun as City Hall
looms in the background.
1951. (Leonard Nadel/
Housing Authority
Collection)

John and Mabel Haufe, proud Bunker Hill homeowners are show visiting together in the front parlor of "Hopecrest," commonly known as the Hildreth Mansion. 1950.

Opposite: Located at 357 S. Hope Street on Bunker Hill and designed by Joseph Cather Newsom, this home was built in 1891 for Rev. Edward T. Hildreth, a Congregational minister. Between 1946 and 1952, John & Mabel Haufe owned the home, renamed "Hopecrest," and lovingly restored it to its former glory. Here, the scaffolding is visible during the restoration. 1949. .

Overleaf: Northeast view of Bunker Hill from the now-demolished Richfield Building, showing off a mix of commercial, residential, and public buildings. The intersection of 5th and Flower Streets is visible, along with Central Library, the Sunkist and Edison Buildings, the backs of apartment buildings like the Touraine (adjacent to the Sunkist) and the Castle Arms (far left). City Hall is in the distance. 1947. (Security Pacific National Bank Collection)

Looking west down 2nd Street from South Bunker Hill Avenue towards the Stanley Apartments at 210 S. Flower Street. The intersection no longer exists and its former location is in between The Broad Museum and Disney Hall. 1949 (Herald Examiner Collection)

Looking east down 3rd Street towards Grand Avenue with Angels Flight in the distance. The Angels Flight Pharmacy was a neighborhood mainstay for over three decades and the intersection was a favorite of comedian Harold Lloyd who used it as a film location in numerous movies. 1955. (William Reagh Collection)

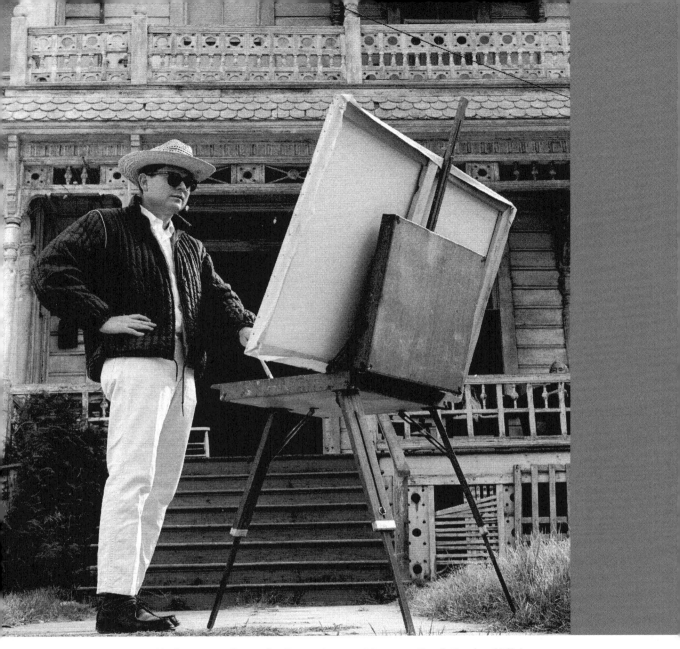

Artist Ben Abril paints in front of a Queen Anne residence on South Bunker Hill Avenue that once belonged to Judge Julius Brousseau. Bunker Hill was popular subject for artists and photographers. 1952. (Roy Hankey Collection)

Opposite: Leo Politi chats with fellow artist Susan Marshall, age 9, and county librarian Mary Rogers Smith in front of "The Castle," located at 325 South Bunker Hill. Politi was one of many artists who visited Bunker Hill in order to document the stately mansions on canvas or in photographs before they were torn down for redevelopment. 1963. (Herald Examiner Collection)

Young residents of the former Argyle Hotel at the corner of 2nd and Olive Streets pose on the rear fire escape. Built sometime in the late 1870s/early 1880s, the Argyle was at one time a respectable establishment that housed a saloon frequented by artists. Various disputes over ownership that began early on left the Argyle to gradually fall into disrepair, eventually rendering it as tenement housing for some of the neighborhood's lower income residents. 1954. (Herald Examiner Collection)

Opposite: The storied "Castle" is shown in its waning years at 325 S. Bunker Hill Avenue. Despite its impending doom, Pearl Mitchman, resident caretaker continues to look after the property as her friend Mrs. Beth Peck looks on. 1966. (Herald Examiner Collection)

ROYBAL
CONGRESS
Elect ALEX P. GARCIA
ASSEMBLYMAN 40TH DIST.
Stop the "Tax Squeeze"
VOTE YES ON #9
LIMIT PROPERTY TAXES
EMBLYMAN

Two men help each other walk past the Hotel Belmont on Hill Street towards 3rd Street, the location of Angels Flight whose days were numbered. 1969. (William Reagh Collection)

A woman named Rose pets a cat near the steps of her home at 246 S. Bunker Hill Avenue.
Ca. 1962. (George Mann Collection)

Well-tended flowers, porch chairs, and filled mailboxes breathe life into the tattered structure on Bunker Hill Avenue. Constructed around 1885, the residence was modest in comparison to the grand mansions on the Avenue, and was converted into a boarding house in 1894, remaining so until it was demolished in the 1960s. Augusta Foss, the daughter of the original owners married Max Heindel, a tenant of the boarding house and founder of the Rosicrucian Fellowship, an "association of Christian mystics." The couple moved to Oceanside in 1910 and established the organization's headquarters on Mount Ecclesia. Ca, 1962. (George Mann Collection)

PART III

Urban "Renewal" Slum Clearance

by DONALD R. SPIVACK

After Bunker Hill's development as an up-scale residential neighborhood overlooking Downtown Los Angeles starting in the 1870s, Los Angeles began developing newer "suburbs" in places such as Pico-Union, Angelino Heights, West Adams and beyond. These neighborhoods attracted the next generation of Angelinos, and were made more desirable as streetcar and inter-urban rail lines expanded, improving access from them to the Central City. The topography of Bunker Hill—steep slopes making walking and vehicular access difficult and a development grid that left many lots unbuildable—eventually led to Bunker Hill's decline, as the City's—and Downtown's—expansion moved under, around and beyond the Hill.[1] The once stately mansions were, over time, converted into apartments and rooming houses, often with poorly built additions, that contributed to residential overcrowding and hastened the deterioration of the housing stock. By the middle of the 20th century it became evident that many of the buildings, especially those of wood or un-reinforced masonry construction, had deteriorated substantially and failed to meet current fire, seismic or electrical code standards. A City of Los Angeles Health Department survey done in preparation for the Redevelopment (Urban Renewal) Plan in December 1955 found 39.62% of the living conditions "extremely substandard," 22.22% "substandard," 19.92% "poor" and only 18.24% "acceptable." A survey by the City Department of Building and Safety in 1957 similarly found 239 out

Opposite: Children play outside their Bunker Hill home. Ca. 1955. (Marion Palm/Housing Authority Collection)

Pages 62-63: - A lone 1956 Ford points towards the Bunker Hill Towers from the graded lots between Hope, Grand, 2nd, and 3rd which are awaiting redevelopment. The block had previously been dissected by South Bunker Hill Avenue and filled with multi-unit dwellings, providing housing to hundreds of residents. The lots eventually became a large parking lot and remained so until the Grand Promenade apartments were constructed on the south end in 1988. Complete redevelopment finally came in 2014 with the opening of The Emerson residential building and the groundbreaking of the Broad Museum. 1971. (William Reagh Collection)

of 395 buildings "dangerous," 1,224 dwelling units in 38 structures illegally occupied, and 4,835 rooms in 271 structures substandard as to room area. Parallel studies showed that the crime rate was twice the City average, the arrest rate eight times the City average and the fire rate per acre nearly nine times the City average."[2]

Meanwhile, in the post World War II era, Los Angeles experienced a significant exodus of households as families flocked to new single family communities in the San Fernando and San Gabriel Valleys, hastened by easy acquisition using various forms of federally funded assistance such as mortgages through the Federal Housing Administration,[3] and eager to experience the freedom that automobile access and a rapidly expanding freeway system gave them. Businesses soon followed, abandoning the Central City as stores and offices also relocated to the suburbs.[4]

To combat the loss of economic activity, the City chose to take advantage of the federal urban renewal program, under the updated National Housing Act of 1949 (PL 81-171), which reinforced nationally efforts to eliminate slums but focused on wholesale clearance of older communities and the construction of new housing in more outlying clusters of "public housing."[5] This reorientation enabled cities, Los Angeles among them, to target the clearance of large areas they designated as "blighted."

The Bunker Hill Urban Renewal Plan was adopted in 1959. It called for removing all of the structures on Bunker Hill, lowering the elevation of the hill, constructing a new road and pedestrian system, installing new utilities and services, and creating a series of large "superblocks" to facilitate the sale of the property to a series of new developers for the area's redevelopment, at an estimated cost of just under $100,000,000. Clearance took place between 1959 and 1964, and required the removal of 7,310 dwelling units[6] and their occupants from 340 residential structures, along with the removal of 132 non-residential structures.[7] While a few of the structures were slated for preservation—relocated to the City's "Heritage Square" area—most were simply demolished.

The initial new construction projects were the Bunker Hill Towers, a complex of approximately 715 apartment and condominium units, and the Union Bank Tower at 5th and Figueroa Streets. To date, over 3,300 residential units have been built on Bunker Hill, along with 8.600,000 square feet of office, 600,000 square feet of retail and 385,000 square feet of cultural space and 2,500 hotel rooms.[8] The area has gone from one which cost the City more to service than it generated in taxes ($754,101 for police, fire and health services in 1957 vs. $106,120)[9] to one that generates over $30,000,000 in net annual revenue to the City today. Much of that has financed over 22,000 units of affordable housing throughout the City.

One positive aspect of the urban renewal program was the ultimate realization that communities such as Bunker Hill, even though made up of very low income individuals and households, nonetheless had a complex internal social structure and cohesiveness. This realization came about from studies done by urban researcher Herbert Gans and colleagues examining the communities in Boston's West End, an area also slated for urban renewal, and one ironically close to the nation's other and, according to some, more famous Bunker Hill.[10] A result of these studies was the 1970 Federal Uniform Relocation Act[11] that laid out and required certain relocation benefits for parties displaced by urban renewal activity; the State of California shortly thereafter adopted a local version for situations (such as under redevelopment) that did not require the use of federal funds. ❧

Once a favorite resting spot of Theodore Roosevelt and William McKinley, the Hotel Melrose was reduced to rubble in 1957. Here, the annex building of the hotel is obliterated while the 1889 Victorian structure awaits its doom. The hotel was replaced with a temporary parking structure which is still standing. 1957. (Security Pacific National Bank Collection)

Built in 1894 by Bernard Sens, a local tailor who provided the police force with their uniforms, this residence eventually operated as a boarding house before becoming the longtime home and office of Dr. James Green. For over thirty years, Green served as the physician for Bunker Hill residents until his death in 1956. The subsequent passing of Green's widow left the house empty and ready for occupancy by the Community Redevelopment Agency who in 1963 moved in and used it as their redevelopment office until 1968. 1967. (William Reagh Collection)

A mother calls to her children sitting on the steps of their apartment on Grand Avenue in the Bunker Hill area. Many may have viewed the neighborhood as a "slum," but many residents fondly called it home. 1948. (Louis Clyde Stoumen/Housing Authority Collection)

Opposite: Young Bunker Hill residents hang out near trash cans and an incinerator. Ca. 1949. (Louis Clyde Stoumen/Housing Authority Collection)

View of the Hotel Gladden and its surroundings at the corner of Olive and 1st Streets. 1952. (Leonard Nadel/Housing Authority Collection)

View of Bunker Hill, looking north along Hope Street towards the Music Center.
Demolition of Bunker Hill houses has already occurred on the west side of the street. 1965.
(Security Pacific National Bank Collection)

Looking north on Bunker Hill Avenue, the Queen Anne architecture of the home visible on the left is a stark contrast to the mid-Century New Formalism applied to the design of the Dorothy Chandler Pavilion at the end of the block. The Dorothy Chandler Pavilion is one of three original buildings comprising the Music Center complex, designed by Welton Becket. The complex, which also includes the Ahamanson Theatre and the Mark Taper Forum was heavily championed by Dorothy Buffum Chandler who sought to bring performing arts to Downtown and marked the first major phase of redevelopment on Bunker Hill. The Pavilion served as home for the Los Angeles Philharmonic's regular season from its opening in 1964 until the Frank Gehry-designed Disney Hall opened in 2003. Ca. 1966. (Security Pacific National Bank Collection)

A man observes a rapidly disappearing Bunker Hill where the tracks of Angels Flight, which had once been surrounded by countless structures, await a similar fate. 1965. (Herald Examiner Collection)

The remnants of the residence known as the "Salt Box" lay smoldering following an arson fire. In an effort to save some part of Bunker Hill for future generations to enjoy, two structures known as the "Salt Box" (339 S. Bunker Hill Avenue) and "The Castle" (325 S. Bunker Hill Avenue) were declared Historic Cultural Monuments 5 and 27, and were later relocated to Heritage Square in the Montecito Heights neighborhood. Unfortunately, both structures became the victims of arson in October 1969. 1969. (Herald Examiner Collection)

An Angels Flight sign and other debris captured during the demolition of the funicular.
1969. (Herald Examiner Collection)

A Bunker Hill outhouse stands its ground during the redevelopment program. In the background is the 42-story Union Bank Building. 1967. (Security Pacific National Bank Collection)

A parking structure running along 1st between Olive Street and Grand Avenue, sits in the shadow of the developing Downtown skyline, composed of: PacBell Tower (1961, now known as the AT&T Madison Complex Tandem Office), Crocker Citizens Bank (1969, now known as 611 Place), United California Bank Building (1973, now known as Aon Center), Arco Plaza towers (1972, now known as City National Plaza), Security Pacific Plaza (1974, now known as Bank of America Plaza), and the Union Bank building (1968). Erected in 1969, the parking structure was designed by engineer Charles Bentley, and modeled after a toy "erector set," meaning it was portable and easy to dismantle and rebuild elsewhere. 2014 marked the 45th anniversary of the temporary structure. 1982. (Roy Hankey Collection)

PART IV

Swinging Sixties

by Adrian Scott Fine

Few would agree on the definitive "L.A. story" as it is a place that defies being easily defined and made up of many different narratives and perspectives. Yet the Los Angeles of the 1960s would certainly rank high, as it epitomizes a time and place when civic pride, prosperity, and optimism were coming together in a way like no other, as a collective force to remake L.A. into something new and distinctly different from the past.

Bunker Hill provided the literal and figurative ground work to make this happen, allowing its leaders at the time to remold it into something more modern and fitting for a city that was desperate to come into its own. The first and most symbolic example of this is the Music Center complex, initially with the opening of the Dorothy Chandler Pavilion in 1964, followed by the Ahmanson Theatre and Mark Taper Forum in 1967. Its indomitable champion and namesake, Mrs. Dorothy "Buff" Chandler, said "[t]he Music Center is many things to many people. To some it represents a magnificent addition to our civic center, a bright new jewel in the diadem of a great city."[1]

Architect Welton Becket called his commission the "single most important element in Southern California's cultural history." As a contemporary expression of classical architecture, the Music Center's New Formalist architecture and its three building complex are united by a central sunken plaza, designed by landscape architecture firm Cornell, Bridgers and Troller. Its innovative design and function for high culture helped cement the Music Center as the west coast equivalent to Manhattan's 1962 Lincoln Center. Both share a similar design aesthetic and narrative of how they came to be through urban renewal.

Opposite: Photograph caption dated October 25, 1965 reads, "Angel's Flight fashions for Angel Week include career bound paisley printed sheer wool skimmer shift." 1965. (Herald Examiner Collection)

Pages 84-85: The Department of Water and Power building (left) and the Dorothy Chandler Pavilion (right) as seen from a parking lot from the South East. 1967. (Security Pacific National Bank Collection)

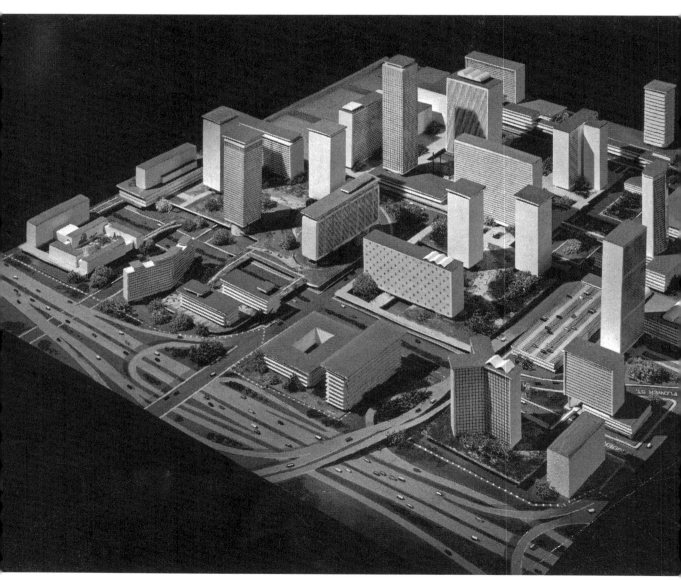

Model shows part of the Bunker Hill redevelopment plan. 1962. (Herald Examiner
Collection)

The Music Center may have been the first but soon would have a new neighbor to the north, the Department of Water and Power (DWP) Building. Built in 1965 and designed by Albert C. Martin and Associates, the seventeen-story Corporate International-style building was intended as "an efficient and unique building in which the city could take pride forever."[2] The building's signature element is concrete floor slabs that extend well beyond the glass enclosure, giving it a greater sense of transparency and horizontal emphasis that downplays the building's overall height.

As a public utility office building, both water and power play dominant roles in the design and on which L.A.'s existence relies. At night it was intended to light up as a conspicuous source of energy and a bright beacon on Bunker Hill. During the day it appears to float within the center of a massive reflecting pool and landscape designed by Cornell, Bridgers and Troller.

Rounding out the 1960s development of Bunker Hill is Union Bank Tower and Plaza, completed in 1968 and designed by Albert C. Martin and Associates. At forty stories, it's the first hi-rise tower to be built within the redevelopment area. Set atop a parking structure plinth and landscaped plaza, it was the model for nearly all of Bunker Hill with a network of similar buildings envisioned. At the time Union Bank CEO Harry Volk said, "Someone had to act as a catalyst in getting that civic improvement project [Bunker Hill's redevelopment] underway."[3]

Union Bank's landscaped plaza is a particular standout feature as a three-acre, sculptural oasis located three stories above grade and designed by noted landscape architect Garrett Eckbo. Grass islands are surrounded by pools of water and linked by a low-slung pedestrian bridge.

While all individually unique, these 1960s-era icons of Bunker Hill set the tone for what followed in the subsequent decades. Each share common traits and a similar vocabulary with car-oriented, independent projects that is primarily internally-focused rather than responding to an existing context. For all these reasons and more, the *new* Bunker Hill that emerged in the 1960s broke with tradition and set a new, exciting direction for L.A.'s future. ঞ

Panoramic view of Downtown Los Angeles, looking east towards Bunker Hill. The Harbor Freeway is in the foreground. While some new construction is taking place near 2nd Street (left), there are still a few of the old Victorian homes seen in the background behind 3rd Street on the right. 1967. (William Reagh Collection)

Architect Robert E. Alexander;
Donald G. Whiteman, President,
City Reconstruction Corp.; Frederick
A. Schnell, Vice-President, Prudential
Insurance Corp.; Mayor Sam Yorty;
and, Z. Wayne Griffin, Chairman,
Community Redevelopment Agency,
view the $60 million high-rise
apartment complex to be named
Bunker Hill Towers. Meant to
draw people to live in the same
neighborhood they worked, only
three of the five Bunker Hill Towers
were constructed, which opened in
1968. In the early 1980s, the units
in the tallest building were converted
to condominiums while the other
two have remained rent-controlled
apartments. 1967. (Herald Examiner
Collection)

Two new buildings going up in the Music Center complex on April 29, 1966. At left is the Mark Taper Forum, and at right is the Ahmanson Theatre. 1966. (Herald Examiner Collection)

The Mark Taper Forum, second unit of the three-unit Music Center complex, is on its way to completion on January 4, 1966, with its upper surface being covered with an 8,640 square foot mural of precast terrazzo. 1966. (Herald Examiner Collection)

Lee Arnold, Music
Center Coordinator,
with Roy Hoover of Los
Angeles County, looking
at the Dorothy Chandler
Pavilion. 1967. (Herald
Examiner Collection)

Crowd of 2,000 waiting to purchase tickets for the opening of the Civic Light Opera at the Ahmanson Theatre. 1967. (Herald Examiner Collection)

Opposite: Future site of a $55 million residential complex on Bunker Hill is pointed out by Lewis Kitchen, to, from left, Robert Alexander, Elmer Hoskine and Kendall Lutes. In the background is the Union Center Building under construction. 1966. (Herald Examiner Collection)

The Union Bank Building and 110 Freeway frame a Bunker Hill in transition where the Department of Water and Power Building (1965) and Dorothy Chandler Pavilion (1964) have been completed, and one of the three Bunker Hill Towers (1968) is under construction. 1968. (William Reagh Collection)

An eight-ton cubical sundial was presented in a ceremony in front of the new 42-story
Union Bank Building, Southern California's tallest office structure, on November 17, 1966.
View is toward the northeast, with the 4th Street overpass and the Dorothy Chandler
Pavilion of the Music Center in view. An undeveloped Bunker Hill is in the distance. 1966.
(Herald Examiner Collection)

Photograph caption dated October 21, 1965 reads, "Fashion seminars by the Broadway, part of Angel Week festivities, will feature two-piece knits for the working girl headquartered in business district of downtown Los Angeles." 1965. (Herald Examiner Collection)

Mrs. Clarence J. Blasiar, general chairman, and Mrs. Fritz B. Burns, press relations chairman and member of the Board of Trustees, stop at Angels Flight news stand to obtain "Extra" announcing eighth annual Angel Ball sponsored by St. Anne's Foundation. 1962. (Herald Examiner Collection)

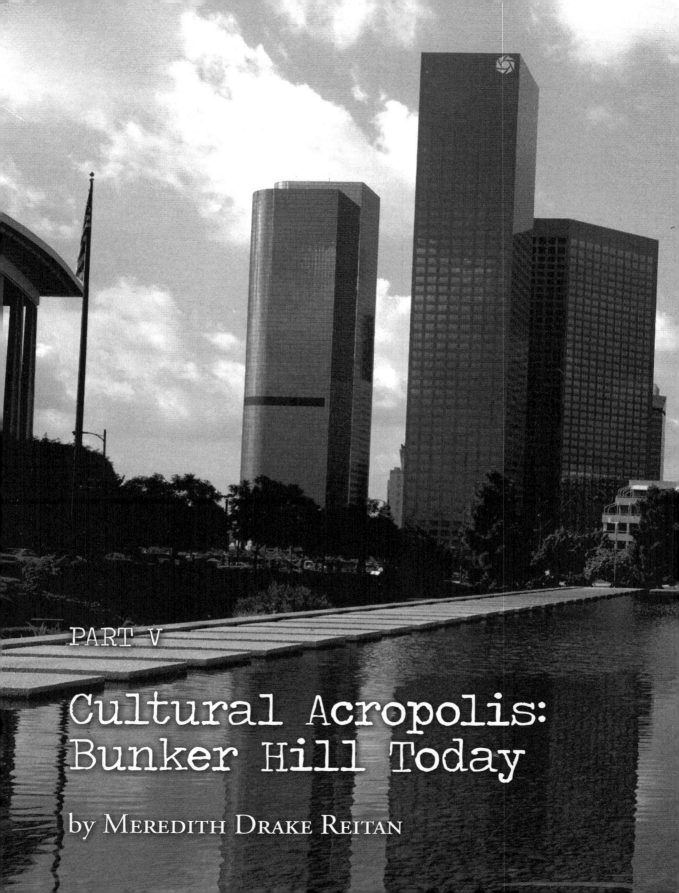

PART V

Cultural Acropolis: Bunker Hill Today

by MEREDITH DRAKE REITAN

There is a wonderful spot on Grand Avenue where the past, present and future of Bunker Hill collide. Standing above the Water Court at the California Plaza, visitors have the reconstructed Angels Flight funicular railway and Los Angeles' early twentieth century financial district at their backs. Before them, the eclectic shapes of the hill's more recent structures battle for visual supremacy.

Amid the skyscrapers and corporate plazas, the triangular skylights and barrel vault of the Museum of Contemporary Art (MOCA) punctuate the foreground. Beyond MOCA, the Broad, which will display the art collection of local philanthropists Eli and Edythe Broad, is now almost complete. Its honeycombed facade allows the faintest sliver of Frank Geary's swooping Disney Concert Hall to be seen behind it. In the distance, the perfectly geometric Department of Water and Power, designed by A.C. Martin, still floats in the background. Not visible from this vantage point, but certainly part of the group, Welton Becket's Music Center, the Colburn School for the Performing Arts and Rafael Moneo's Cathedral of Our Lady of the Angels can be found a little further along Grand Avenue. Where once the Music Center sat alone in an "urban renewal wasteland, set off . . . by forbidding streets only the swift would attempt to cross on foot," today, Angelinos enjoy the crown of downtown LA's "glittering art Mecca."[1]

Credit for the most recent development goes to the Grand Avenue Authority, a joint powers authority involving the Community Redevelopment Agency and the County of Los Angeles. However, as with most large-scale

Opposite: Judy Cotter sits on the stairs, in-between the Angels Flight railroad tracks. A sign on the left side of the tracks reads, "Park Hours, Winter 9:00 AM to 5:00 PM, Summer 9:00 AM to 8:00 PM, No Loitering," and another sign below reads, "Gates locked when red light on." 2005. (Thomas K. Meyer)

Pages 106-107: Looking south from the water courtyard of the General Office Building of the Department of Water and Power, located at 111 N. Hope Street. 1986. (William Reagh Collection)

construction projects, the stage for this particular scene was set much earlier when the current assembly was simply a glint in the eye of the city's twentieth-century planners.

The area that would eventually become this spectacular architectural parade was for many years a vacant "weed-choked, litter-strewn" hole in the ground.[2] Twenty-four years after the old mansions were removed, the CRA initiated plans for the last uncommitted land on Bunker Hill. Described as the largest redevelopment project in city history, a number of development teams competed for the opportunity to rebuild on the tabula rasa. One of the most interesting proposals was submitted by local developers, Maguire Partners who gave some of the worlds best-known architects their "own sandbox to play in."[3] Overseen by architect Barton Myers and master planned by UCLA's Harvey Perloff, the Maguire proposal included a signature tower by Cesar Pelli, landscape elements by Lawrence Halprin and contributions from Charles Moore, Hugh Hardy, Ricardo Legoretta, Deborah Sussman and Frank Gehry.[4]

While an apparently impressive submission, the Maguire proposal was described as impractical and the project was given instead to the more pragmatic Bunker Hill Associates. The design team included Arthur Erickson, Kamnitzer & Cotton and Gruen Associates who envisioned more than 3 million square feet of offices, about 700 residential units, movie and entertainment outlets and 5 acres of park space. As with the Maguire plan, the new development also included space for a museum of contemporary art.

City leaders were particularly enthusiastic about the inclusion of the museum and quickly approved the project. After lengthy and occasionally heated discussions about the design, the red sandstone building designed by Arata Isozaki in collaboration with Gruen Associates was opened to the public in December 1986 as an "oasis of low-rise tranquility."[5]

MOCA's success made additional cultural projects more attractive, including the expansion of the Music Center. In the early 1980s, six resident performing arts companies were housed at the Dorothy Chandler Pavillion which also hosted the Academy Awards.[6] First considered in 1968, the leadership of the Music Center intended to build on land immediately to the south, on a site known as Parcel K at First and Hope Street. Los Angeles County, who owned the lot preferred to use the space for commercial development and recommended a location on the Civic Center Mall, suggesting that the mall location "crowns the confluence of downtown's commercial, cultural and civic sectors."[7] Architectural drawings were completed by Barton Myers in 1985 for a structure that would span Grand Avenue. Music Center leaders were apparently horrified and argued that building on the civic center site would cost millions more than construction on Parcel K.

After a two year stand-off, the dispute was settled in early 1987 when Lillian B. Disney offered a gift of $50 million in honor of her late husband, Walt Disney. A condition of the gift was to locate any new Music Center buildings on Parcel K. The design competition for the Walt Disney Concert Hall was described as a "yardstick" of contemporary international architecture. Four finalists were selected, including Frank Gehry, whose initial entry was of "sculpted limestone-clad forms" with a glass conservatory serving as the entry foyer. The conservatory was designed to make the space "a living room for the city". Gehry, clearly the local favorite, was personally selected by Lillian Disney in December 1988.[8] Scheduled to open in fall 1993, due to significant cost overruns, the building did not open until 2003.

The new towers on Grand Avenue offer a poetic "rush of verticality" and are evidence of Los Angeles' strategic role in the global economy.[9] However, it is the various cultural venues that truly set today's Bunker Hill apart. With the recently opened Grand Park that transformed the underutilized Civic Center Mall into a lively, if somewhat overly programmed, community space, recent redevelopment efforts have started to stitch together a community that many thought was lost when the bulldozers arrived in the early 1960s. ❧

Looking south from the water courtyard of the General Office Building of the Department of Water and Power, located at 111 N. Hope Street. 1972. (William Reagh Collection)

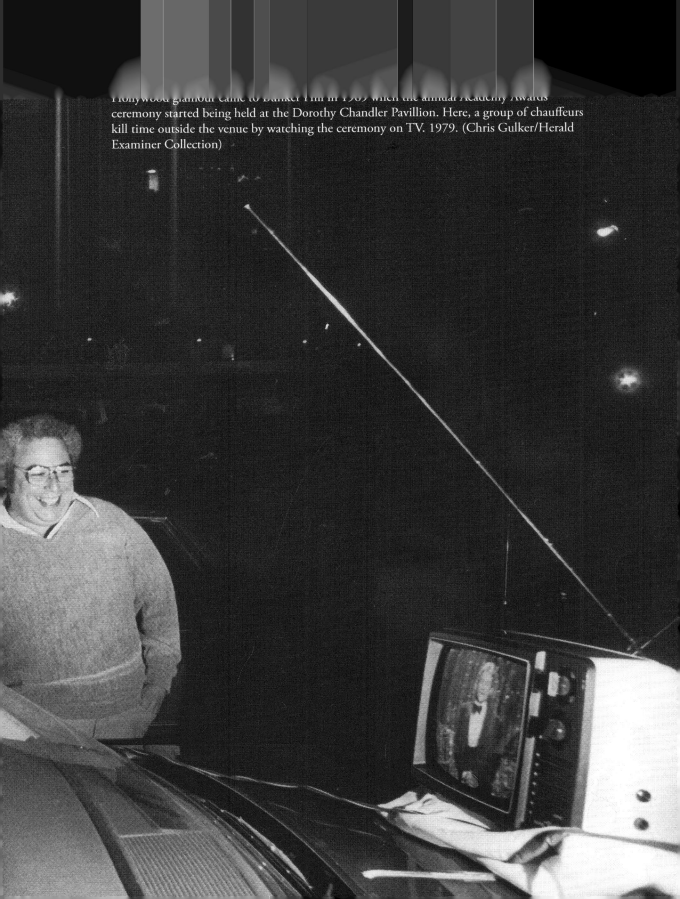

Hollywood glamour came to Bunker Hill in 1969 when the annual Academy Awards ceremony started being held at the Dorothy Chandler Pavillion. Here, a group of chauffeurs kill time outside the venue by watching the ceremony on TV. 1979. (Chris Gulker/Herald Examiner Collection)

View from the California Plaza of buildings located on Bunker Hill. 1989. (William Reagh Collection)

Panoramic view of the Bonaventure Hotel and the Union Bank Building, looking southwest from Hope Street near the Security Pacific Bank Building (right) on Bunker Hill. The sculpture seen in the courtyard is called *Four Arches,* which was created by Alexander Calder in 1974. 1989. (William Reagh Collection)

Two unidentified people chat at the steps of the Watercourt at California Plaza. The Watercourt Performance Plaza was designed by WET Design with collaboration from Arthur Erickson Architects. 2000. (Marissa Roth/Los Angeles Neighborhoods Collection)

Opposite: Two people chat on Grand Avenue. Several high-rise buildings can be seen in the background, the most prominent is the PacBell Tower (C. Day Woodford and Leonard Bernard, AKA Woodford & Bernard, Archs, 1961). 2000. (Marissa Roth/Los Angeles Neighborhoods Collection)

Exterior view of the Museum of Contemporary Art, with a view of the Claes Oldenburg and Coosje van Bruggen sculpture titled *Knife/Ship II*. 1996. (Marissa Roth/Los Angeles Neighborhoods Collection)

Opposite: Photograph caption dated December 13, 1984 reads, "While many parts of the Los Angeles area were blacked out, DWP workers were burning the midnight oil at still-lighted headquarters off Harbor Freeway." 1984. (James Ruebsamen/Herald Examiner Collection)

Architect Frank Gehry standing next to his model of the new Disney Hall to be built on the corner of Grand Avenue and First Street. 1994. (John Chacon)

Men working with some wood, but mostly steel bars, on the Colburn School construction project at 2nd and Hill Streets. The Colburn School is a music, dance, and drama school. 2005. (Gary Leonard Collection)

His Eminence Roger Cardinal Mahony standing in front a section of the new Cathedral of Our Lady of the Angels' campanile. Excavation for the foundations of the Cathedral, designed by the renowned Spanish architect, Jose Rafael Moneo, began in May 1999. 2001. (Gary Leonard Collection)

Opposite: Corner view of 5th and Olive Streets. Photo shows the Southern California Gas Company building, the SBC building (Madison Complex) with a painted mural by Frank Stella (*Dusk*, 1991) on one wall, the California Plaza building in the background, and a corner of the Biltmore Hotel on the left. 2005. (Gary Leonard Collection)

Contributor Biographies

As Director of Advocacy for the Los Angeles Conservancy, **Adrian Scott Fine** oversees the organization's outreach, advocacy and response on key preservation issues within the greater Los Angeles area. The Conservancy is the largest local nonprofit preservation organization in the country. Previously Mr. Fine was with the National Trust for Historic Preservation and Indiana Landmarks. He graduated from Ball State University with degrees in Urban Planning and Development, Environmental Design and Historic Preservation. In 2014 he was selected as a Fitch Mid-Career Fellow by the James Marston Fitch Charitable Foundation for the project, "Picking up the Pieces: Preserving Urban Renewal's Modern Legacy." He is a founding member of Docomomo US/SoCal.

Nathan Marsak is a Los Angeles historian whose wide-ranging work includes interpreting and advocating for the architectural and cultural history of lost 19th and 20th Century Los Angeles, through such history blogs as 1947project, On Bunker Hill and In SRO Land, his monograph on the city's neon signage and campaign to Save the 76 Balls. Nathan was named the Los Angeles Visionary Association (LAVA) Visionary of the Year for 2015.

Merry Ovnick is the editor of the *Southern California Quarterly*. She is a professor emeritus of history at California State University, Northridge, where she taught urban history, Los Angeles history, and interdisciplinary courses on urban policy. She is the immediate past president of the Society of Architectural Historians/Southern California Chapter and the author of *Los Angeles: The End of the Rainbow* (1994), a social and architectural history of this region.

Dr. Meredith Drake Reitan is a planning historian whose work has been published in the *Journal of Planning History* and in an edited volume for Planners Press. She serves as the Associate Dean of Fellowships at the University of Southern California and as an adjunct associate professor in USC's Sol Price School of Public Policy where she teaches classes on planning theory and public space. Her blog, called the LAvenuesProject, uses the thousands of mundane decisions that define the look and feel of LA streets to talk about the long history of the city as a planned environment. She is also currently at work on a book about the history of the Los Angeles Civic Center. Dr. Drake Reitan has a PhD and Masters in Planning from USC, a Graduate Certificate in Visual Studies from USC, and a B.A. in Spanish Literature from the University of California at Santa Cruz.

Christina Rice is the Senior Librarian of the Los Angeles Public Library Photo Collection, a position she has held for five of her nine years with the library. She graduated from Cal State Fullerton with a BA in Communications, and obtained a Masters of Library and Information Science from San Jose State University. She is the author of *Ann Dvorak: Hollywood's Forgotten Rebel* (University Press of Kentucky, 2013) and has written multiple issues of the My Little Pony comic book series (IDW Publishing). She lives in North Hollywood with her husband, writer Joshua Hale Fialkov, their daughter, two dogs, and a disgruntled cat.

Emma Roberts has held the position of Librarian III / Subject Specialist in the Art, Music & Recreation and Rare Books Departments at Los Angeles Public Library since 2005. Originally from the UK, she received her BA in Art History from the University of Warwick, and her Masters in Library and Information Studies from Loughborough University. She is the 2015 Chair of the Los Angeles Preservation Network (LAPNet) which addresses the preservation needs of librarians, archivists, conservators and records managers working in the Los Angeles area, and serves as an Editorial Advisory Board member for the journal *Reference Services Review: reference and instructional services for libraries in the digital age.*

Heritage conservationist **Trudi Sandmeier** is a native Angeleno with a passion for the history and built environment of Los Angeles. She is an Associate Professor of Practice and the Director of Graduate Programs in Heritage Conservation for the USC School of Architecture. She previously spent almost eleven years with the Los Angeles Conservancy, holding the titles of Preservation Advocate, Broadway Initiative Coordinator, and Director of Education.

Donald R. Spivack is a planning and urban development consultant with over 40 years of professional transportation, land use planning and urban redevelopment work in local government. He currently consults with the Los

Angeles Neighborhood Land Trust on developing funding for parks and open space in under-served inner city communities in Los Angeles and with the Los Angeles Collaborative for Environmental Health and Justice, a consortium of community-based organizations, on a policy to reduce adverse effects of industrial pollution resulting from concentrated industrial uses in densely developed neighborhoods. He is also an adjunct professor in the Sol Price School of Social Policy at the University of Southern California, and sits on the Advisory Board of the Los Angeles River Revitalization Corporation, a local economic development entity (which he helped create) targeting water quality and habitat improvements matched with sustainable urban development. In addition to transportation system development and planning work in Boston, Detroit, Philadelphia and Washington, DC, Mr. Spivack served on staff of the Community Redevelopment Agency of the City of Los Angeles (CRA/LA), from which he retired in 2010 as Deputy Chief of Operations and Policy, where he was responsible for developing long-range redevelopment and revitalization policies and strategies, including land use, industrial development, transportation and transit oriented development, job development, business attraction, open space and financing options in an era of declining tax revenues. While at the CRA/LA, Mr. Spivack was also in charge of drafting, in conjunction with the Los Angeles Department of City Planning, an updated Industrial Land Use Policy for the City, and CRA/LA's Healthy Neighborhoods Policy and Neighborhood Conservation Strategy, both of which dealt with fostering appropriate economic development in ways that were both protective and sustainable. Earlier in his tenure at the CRA/LA Mr. Spivack managed several of the agency's redevelopment project areas including those in Downtown Los Angeles and along several major transit corridors. Mr. Spivack holds a BA in Architecture from the University of Pennsylvania and a Masters of City Planning from Yale University.

Endnotes

PART I.
EARLY SUBURB

1 William David Estrada, *The Los Angeles Plaza: Sacred and Contested Space* (Austin: University of Texas Press, 2008), 30, 44; William Mason and Jeanne Duque, "Los Angeles: Living Symbol of Our Past," *Terra* (Winter 1981.

2 O.C. Ord, Lt. USA and Wm. R. Hutton, *Plan de la Ciudad de Los Angeles, City Map No. 1*, 1849,and O. C. Ord, Henry Hancock, and George Hansen, *Map of the City of Los Angeles*, c. 1875 in Glenn Creason, *Los Angeles in Maps* (New York: Rizzoli, 2010), 32-33, 38-39.

3 E.S. Glover, *Birds Eye View of Los Angeles, California, Looking South to the Pacific Ocean...*(A. L. Bancroft, Publisher, 1877) in Creason, *Los Angeles in Maps*, 44-45.

4 The US Census figures for the City of Los Angeles were 11,183 in 1880, 50,395 in 1890.

5 Sanborn Fire Insurance Maps for Los Angeles, California, 1888, pages 19-22, 27.

6 Glenn S. Dumke, *The Boom of the Eighties in Southern California* (San Marino, CA: Huntington Library, 1963), 49.

7 Clark Davis, *Company Men: White-Collar Life and Corporate Cultures in Los Angeles, 1892-1941* (Baltimore: The Johns Hopkins University Press, 2000.

8 Sanborn Fire Insurance Maps for Los Angeles, California, 1894, pages 1-3.

9 Rick Rosen, et al, "A Guide to the Restoration and Reconstruction of Angels Flight," (pamphlet) (Los Angeles Conservancy, 1995; "Angels Flight Went Out on a Limb," *Los Angeles Times*, October 11, 2013; John H. Welborne, "The Seven Operators of the Angels Flight Railway," (Los Angeles City Historical Society, May 2010): 7-8; Leonard Pitt and Dale Pitt, *Los Angeles A to Z* (Berkeley: University of California Press, 1997), 104; Gernot Kuehn, *View of Los Angeles* (Los Angeles: Portriga, 1978), 30

PART II.

FLOURISHING NEIGHBORHOOD

1 "Bunker Hill Property Owners Hit Proposal C," *Los Angeles Times*, April 1, 1951, B3.

PART III.
URBAN "RENEWAL" SLUM CLEARANCE

1 Kawaratani, Yukio. *Reluctant Samurai: Memoirs of an Urban Planner*. Self-published manuscript, 2007, p. 171. See also statement attributed to C. C. Bigelow, president of Southwestern Investment Corporation, in 1929, that Bunker Hill is a "barrier to progress in the business district of Los Angeles, preventing natural expansion westward ... the removal or regrading of Bunker Hill is practically a necessity." Cited in Anderton, Francis, Editor. *Grand Illusion: A Story of Ambition, and its Limits, on LA's Bunker Hill*. USC Pamphlet Series CEZI/001, 2011, p. 36.

2 Reports to City Council cited in "In Re Redevelopment Plan for Bunker Hill, 61 Cal. 2d", February 27, 1964.

3 Jackson, Kenneth T. *Crabgrass Frontier: the Suburbanization of the United States*. Oxford University Press, 1985, pp 203-209

4 See, for example, Gish, Todd, "Challenging the Myth of an Unplanned Los Angeles" in Sloane, David C., Editor. *Planning Los Angeles*. American Planning Association, 2012, pp. 29-30.

5 Title 1, Slum Clearance and Community Development and Redevelopment of the National Housing Act of 1949 specifically provided financial assistance and other incentives to local jurisdictions to undertake the elimination of areas they designated as "blighted." California had adopted its own legislative authorization for redevelopment in 1945. The National Housing Act of 1954 expanded slum clearance to promote economic revitalization.

6 Community Redevelopment Agency of the City of Los Angeles, CA. Implementation Plan for the Bunker Hill Redevelopment Project FY2010-FY2012. CRA/LA, December 17, 2009, p 1.

7 Ordinance adopting the Bunker Hill Urban Renewal Plan section 5, cited in "In Re Redevelopment Plan for Bunker Hill, 61 Cal. 2d", February 27, 1964.

8 Community Redevelopment Agency of the City of Los Angeles, CA. Implementation Plan for the Bunker Hill Redevelopment Project FY2010-FY2012. CRA/LA, December 17, 2009, p 2.

9 Ordinance adopting the Bunker Hill Urban Renewal Plan section 4, cited in "In Re Redevelopment Plan for Bunker Hill, 61 Cal. 2d", February 27, 1964.

10 Gans, Herbert J. *The Urban Villagers: Group and Class in the Life of Italian-Americans.* Free Press, 1982.

11 49 CFR Part 24. See also California counterpart, California Government Code Sections 7260-7277 (1969).

PART IV.
SWINGING SIXTIES

1 Music Center: A Living Memorial to Peace. *Los Angeles Times.* December 6, 1964

2 Kanner, Diane. AC Martin Partners: One Hundred Years of Architecture: Los Angeles: AC Martin Partners, Inc. and Balcony Press, 2006; 47.

3 Union Bank: 150 Years of History. 2014

PART V.
CULTURAL ACROPOLIS: BUNKER HILL TODAY

1 Wilson, William "MOCA: A Downtown Oasis in a Former Wasteland" *Los Angeles Times* August 25, 1985 pg. U92; Kaplan, Sam Hall "Urban Visions of the Future" *Los Angeles* December 2, 1984 pg. W5

2 Vollmer, Ted "California Plaza Ground Breaking Won't Bury Questions" *Los Angeles Times* October 11, 1983 pg. C1; Kaplan, Sam Hall, "City's Most Ambitious Redevelopment Project: Plaza Design Improved" *Los Angeles Times*, October 2, 1983

3 Dreyfuss, John, "Last Project on Bunker Hill Holds Key to Downtown's Future" *Los Angeles Times* May 18, 1980 pg. K1

4 Dreyfuss, John, "Last Project on Bunker Hill Holds Key to Downtown's Future" *Los Angeles Times* May 18, 1980 pg. K1; Whiteson, Leon "An Architect's Architect Succumbs to Charms of Los Angeles" *Los Angeles Times* February 13, 1988

5 Champlin, Charles "MOCA: A Sign of Changes on the Hill" *Los Angeles Times* May 17, 1986 pg. F1

6 Vollmer, Ted "Music Center Dispute Not Over Need to Expand—but Where?" *Los Angeles Times* February 22, 1987 pg. B1

7 Whiteson, Leon "Harmony on the Hill with Disney Hall" *Los Angeles Times*, April 29, 1988 pg. F1

8 Kaplan, Sam Hall "A Competition in Spirit of Disney" *Los Angeles Times*, December 11, 1988 pg. 12

9 Sanders, James "Look at Downtown, the New Los Angeles" *Los Angeles Times*, February 16, 1986 pg. 217

About the Photo Collection

The Los Angeles Public Library (LAPL) began collecting photographs sometime before World War II and had a collection of about 13,000 images by the late 1950s. In 1981, when Los Angeles celebrated its 200th birthday, Security Pacific National Bank gave its noted collection of historical photographs to the people of Los Angeles to be archived at the Central Library. Since then, LAPL has been fortunate to receive other major collections, making the Library a resource worldwide for visual images.

Notable collections include the "photo morgues" of the *Los Angeles Herald Examiner* and *Valley Times* newspapers, the Kelly-Holiday mid-century collection of aerial photographs, the Works Progress Administration/Federal Writers Project collection, the Luther Ingersoll Portrait Collection, along with the landmark *Shades of L.A.*, an archive of images representing the contemporary and historic diversity of families in Los Angeles. Images were chosen from family albums and copied in a project sponsored by Photo Friends.

The Los Angeles Public Library Photo Collection also includes the works of individual photographers, including Ansel Adams, Herman Schultheis, William Reagh, Ralph Morris, Lucille Stewart, Gary Leonard, Stone Ishimaru, Carol Westwood, and Rolland Curtis.

Over 100,000 images from these collections have been digitized and are available to view through the LAPL website at **http://photos.lapl.org.**

About Photo Friends

Formed in 1990, Photo Friends is a nonprofit organization that supports the Los Angeles Public Library's Photograph Collection and History & Genealogy Department. Our goal is to improve access to the collections and promote them through programs, projects, exhibits, and books such as this one.

We are an enthusiastic group of photographers, writers, historians, business people, politicians, academics, and many others—all bonded by our passion for photography, history, and Los Angeles.

Since 1994, Photo Friends has presented a series called *The Photographer's Eye,* which spotlights local photographers and their work. These talks are presented bi-monthly. In 2011, Photo Friends inaugurated *L.A. in Focus,* a lecture series that features images drawn primarily from the Photo Collection. We have presented programs on L.A. crime, the San Fernando Valley, Kelly-Holiday aerial photographs, and L.A.'s themed environments, and L.A.'s music history, among others.

With initial funding from the Ralph M. Parsons Foundation, Photo Friends sponsored *L.A. Neighborhoods Project* by commissioning photographers to create a visual record of the neighborhoods of Los Angeles during the early part of the 21st century (all now part of the collection). To ensure the Library's Collection will continue to reflect such an important part of Los Angeles's history, a generous grant enabled Photo Friends to hire five contemporary photographers to document present-day industrial L.A. These images have become part of LAPL's permanent collection and are available through the library's photo database. Photo Friends also curates photography exhibits on display in the History Department.

Photo Friends is a membership organization. Please consider becoming a member and helping us in our work to preserve and promote L.A.'s rich photographic resource. All proceeds from the sale of this book go to support Photo Friends' programs.

Society for American City and Regional Planning History (SACRPH) is an interdisciplinary organization dedicated to promoting scholarship on the planning of cities and metropolitan regions over time, and to bridging the gap between the scholarly study of cities and the practice of urban planning.

Thank You!

Special thanks to Kim Creighton, Mitch Browning, Giovanna Mannino, and the Society for American City and Regional Planning History

Bunker Hill in the Rearview Mirror:
The Rise, Fall, and Rise Again of an Urban Neighborhood
Edited by Christina Rice and Emma Roberts
Essays by Merry Ovnick, Nathan Marsak, Donald Spivack, Adrian Scott Fine, Meredith Drake Reitan

This book accompanies the exhibition, *Bunker Hill in the Rearview Mirror: The Rise, Fall, and Rise Again of an Urban Neighborhood,* which opened at Central Library in May 2015.

Published by:
Photo Friends of the Los Angeles Public Library
c/o Future Studio
P.O. Box 292000
Los Angeles, CA 90029

www.photofriends.org

Designed by Amy Inouye, Future Studio Los Angeles

Special quantity discounts available when purchased in bulk by corporations, organizations, or groups. Please contact Photo Friends at: **photofriendsla@gmail.com**

ISBN-13: 978-0692703427

Printed in the United States

Looking south at Hill Street from Temple before the Hill Street Tunnel was bored.
Although the streets are unpaved, streetcar tracks are visible in the foreground. 1908.
(Security Pacific National Bank Collection)

75778637R00075

Made in the USA
San Bernardino, CA
05 May 2018